Level 1

CW01655265

GOLDILOCKS and the THREE BEARS

Text
Sarah Bisson

Illustrations
Marygribouille

Belin:
ÉDUCATION

How to read this book...

Collection dirigée par Séraphine Lansonneur,
formatrice en anglais à l'INSPE de Paris

Dossier pédagogique de Séraphine Lansonneur

SUMMARY

Before the story

The story

After the story

THE CHARACTERS

My name is **Goldilocks**.
I am curious, energetic
and adventurous.

golden hair

teddy bear

This is my **mum**.

This is **the Bear family**.

Daddy Bear

Mummy Bear

Baby Bear

THE PLACES

My house

The forest

Goldilocks and the Three Bears

Goldilocks: Bye mum!

Mum: Bye Goldilocks! Come back for dinner!

Goldilocks: The forest is beautiful!
Teddy bear, look at the flowers, the animals...

Oh, look, a house! It's beautiful!

Who lives here? Let's go in!

Look, it's the **kitchen**. I'm **hungry**!

Let's eat!

This soup is too **hot**!

This soup is too **cold**!

This soup is just perfect! Yummy!

I'm **bored**. I'm bored. I'm BORED.

Oh, what's this?

Look, it's the living room!

Let's sit!

This **chair** is too **high**!

This chair
is too **low**!

This chair is just perfect!

Oooops... Sorry!

I'm **tired** now! Oh, what's this?

Look, it's the bedroom!

Let's sleep!

This **bed**

is too hard.

This bed is

too soft.

This bed is just perfect.

Sweet dreams, teddy bear!

Daddy Bear: Ah, back home!

Mummy Bear: Oh, the door is wide open!

Baby Bear: I'm afraid!

Daddy Bear:

My **spoon** is dirty!

Mummy Bear:

MY spoon

is dirty!

Baby Bear:

And MY spoon is dirty!

Where's my soup?

Daddy Bear:

My chair is untidy!

Mummy Bear:

MY chair is untidy!

Baby Bear:

And MY chair

is broken!

Daddy Bear:

My bed is messy!

Mummy Bear:

MY bed is messy!

Baby Bear:

And MY bed...

Baby Bear: A girl? And a **tiny** baby bear? In MY bed?

Goldilocks: What? Bears?

Help! Help!

I'm scared!

Daddy Bear: Don't worry, we are nice bears.

Mummy Bear: What's your name, little girl?

Goldilocks: Wow, you can talk! My name is Goldilocks.

Baby Bear: What's your name, tiny baby bear?

Goldilocks: He can't talk. He's not a talking bear. He's a TEDDY bear.

Baby Bear: I'm hungry!

Goldilocks: Come to my house!

My mum has prepared dinner.

Mmm!
Chomp! Chomp!
Yum! Yum!

Mummy Bear: I'm happy!

Daddy Bear: I'm happy too.

Now, Baby Bear has got a friend.

GIVE YOUR OPINION!

The story is...

★★★★ excellent ★★★ good ★ poor

Why? interesting boring funny sad

My favourite character is...

Goldilocks | Baby Bear | Mummy Bear | Daddy Bear

Why? curious courageous scary funny nice

My favourite page is...

Why? the best moment the suspense

My favourite words are...

MORE FUN!

Help the bears find their things!

2 Count the animals!

MORE FACTS!

Which is your favourite?

2 Match each famous bear and his country.

a. India | b. The United States | c. England

1. Paddington

2. Baloo

3. Yogi Bear

VOCABULARY

bear / teddy bear

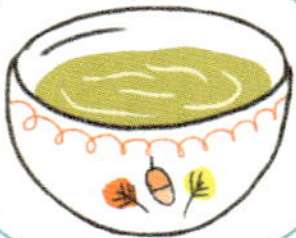

big

small

tiny

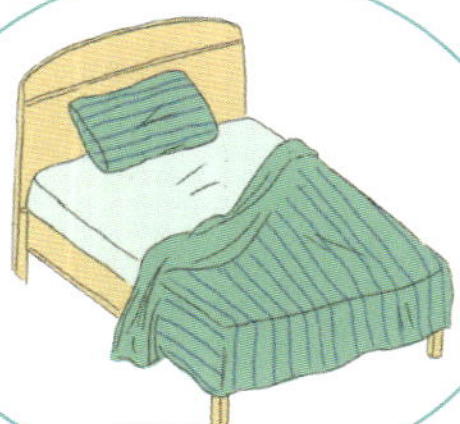

bed

bored

chair

cold

hot

high

low

spoon

hungry

tired

kitchen

Answers

p. 34 :

p. 35 : There are 9 animals.
p. 37 : 1c, 2a, 3b.

Credits

Des ressources pédagogiques gratuites sur myenglishfactory.fr

Version audio intégrale des textes

Affiches pour la classe

Guide pédagogique complet

- déroulé pas à pas des séances d'écoute et de lecture
- fiches didactiques sur l'enseignement de l'anglais pour chaque niveau
- *flashcards* de vocabulaire
- fiches d'activités

170 bis, boulevard du Montparnasse, 75680 Paris cedex 14
ISBN 979-10-358-2829-5
Loi 49-956 du 16 juillet 1949 sur les publications destinées à la jeunesse

IMPRIM'VERT®

La pâte à papier utilisée pour la fabrication du papier de cet ouvrage provient de forêts certifiées et gérées durablement.

Imprimé en France par Pollina
N° d'imprimeur : 46003 - Dépôt légal : mars 2023
N° d'édition : 03582829-01